Amphibian Babies

Catherine Veitch

Heinemann
LIBRARY
Chicago, Illinois

© 2013 Heinemann Library
an imprint of Capstone Global Library, LLC
Chicago, Illinois

To contact Capstone Global Library please phone
800-747-4992, or visit our website
www.capstonepub.com

Edited by Daniel Nunn, Rebecca Rissman,
and Catherine Veitch
Designed by Cynthia Della-Rovere
Picture research by Ruth Blair
Production by Victoria Fitzgerald
Originated by Capstone Global Library

Library of Congress Cataloging-in-Publication Data

Veitch, Catherine.
  Amphibian babies / Catherine Veitch.
     pages cm.—(Animal babies)
  Includes bibliographical references and index.
  ISBN 978-1-4329-7491-6 (hb)
  ISBN 978-1-4329-8416-8 (pb)
  1. Amphibians—Infancy—Juvenile literature. I. Title.
  QL644.2.V447 2013
  597.813'92—dc23   2012033021

Image Credits
Getty Images: Robert Ellis, 12; Nature Picture Library:
BERNARD CASTELEIN, 14, Doug Wechsler, 8, Edwin
Giesbers, 16, Fabio Liverani, 13, Inaki Relanzon, 20,
Nature Production, cover, 1, 10, Philippe Clement, 17,
Rod Williams, 21, Todd Pusser, 6, Visuals Unlimited, 7;
Shutterstock: Bo Valentino, 5 (top right), Cathy Keifer, 19,
Dirk Ercken, 11 (left), 11 (right), 23 (middle), DJTaylor,
22 (top), Doug Wechsler, 23 (bottom), Eric Isselée, 22
(all bottom), ethylalkohol, 18, Ian Grainger, back cover,
9, 23 (top), ihsan Gercelman, 4 (left), Matteo photos, 4
(right), Melinda Fawver, 5 (bottom left), Ryan M. Bolton,
5 (bottom right), Svetlana Foote, 15, Tom C Amon, 3, 5
(top left)

We would like to thank Michael Bright for his invaluable
help in the preparation of this book.

Every effort has been made to contact copyright holders
of material reproduced in this book. Any omissions will
be rectified in subsequent printings if notice is given to
the publisher.

Contents

What Is an Amphibian?

Amphibians live on land.
Amphibians also live in water.

Frogs and toads are amphibians.
Newts and salamanders are
amphibians.

How Are Most Baby Amphibians Born?

eggs

Most amphibians lay their eggs in water.

Some amphibians lay their eggs on land.

spawn

Most amphibians lay their eggs in a jelly. This is called spawn.

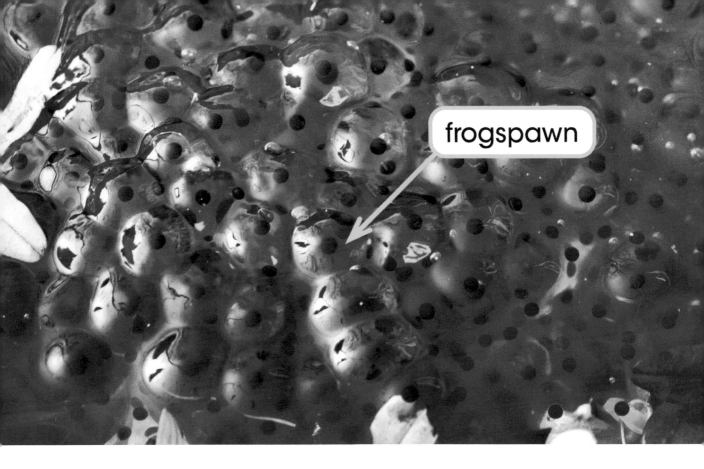

frogspawn

A frog's egg jelly is called
frogspawn.

larva

A larva hatches from each egg.

larva

parent

The larva does not look like
its parent.

Growing Up

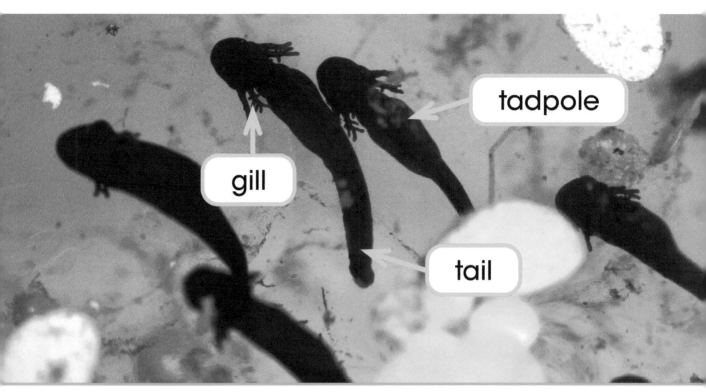

gill

tadpole

tail

Frog larvae are called tadpoles.
Tadpoles have tails and gills.

The tadpoles grow legs.

The tadpoles lose their tails and gills. The tadpoles grow into froglets.

The froglets grow into frogs. The
frogs are ready to leave the water.

Live Amphibian Babies

Some amphibians give birth to
live babies.

adult

baby

Many of these amphibian babies look like the adults.

Caring for Babies

Most baby amphibians look after themselves. They find a new home.

They catch their own food.

eggs

Some amphibians care for
their eggs.

tadpole

Some amphibians care for their larvae.

Life Cycle of an Amphibian

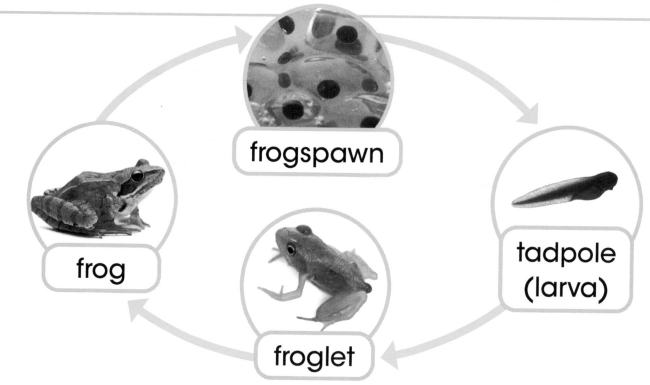

frogspawn

tadpole (larva)

froglet

frog

A life cycle shows the different stages of an animal's life. This is the life cycle of a frog.

Picture Glossary

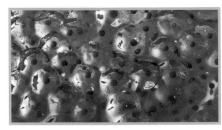

frogspawn frogs' eggs in a jelly

larva stage some amphibians have when they first hatch. More than one is larvae.

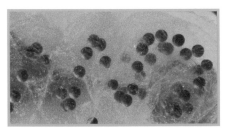

spawn eggs of some animals such as frogs that are in a jelly

Index

Notes to Parents and Teachers

Before reading

Show children a collection of photos and videos of amphibians. National Geographic and PBS are useful websites. Explain what an amphibian is and discuss the characteristics of amphibians.

After reading

- Mount photos of adult and baby amphibians on note cards and play games of concentration where the children have to match a baby amphibian with its parent. Model the correct pairs first.

- Ask children to label the parts of an amphibian: for example, head, feet, tail, scales.

- Look at page 22 and discuss the life cycle stages of an amphibian. Mount photos of the eggs, larvae, baby, and adult stages and ask children to put the photos in order. Encourage children to draw a life cycle of a human to compare. Compare how different amphibians care for their babies. Discuss the care human babies need.

- To extend children's knowledge, the amphibians are as follows: frogs: p. 4; salamander eggs: p. 6; salamander: p. 7; toad eggs: p. 8; frogspawn: p. 9; salamander larva: p. 10; crested newt: p. 11; frog tadpole: pp. 12, 13; frog: pp. 14, 15; lizard: p. 16; salamander: p. 17; frog: pp. 18, 19; toad: p. 20; poison arrow frog: p. 21.